Handbook for Teachers of Non-Native Speakers of English

to accompany

The Art of Public Speaking

Seventh Edition

Stephen E. Lucas
University of Madison-Wisconsin

McGraw Hill

Boston   Burr Ridge, IL   Dubuque, IA   Madison, WI   New York   San Francisco   St. Louis
Bangkok   Bogotá   Caracas   Kuala Lumpur   Lisbon   London   Madrid   Mexico City
Milan   Montreal   New Delhi   Santiago   Seoul   Singapore   Sydney   Taipei   Toronto

McGraw-Hill Higher Education
A Division of The McGraw-Hill Companies

Handbook for Teachers of Non-Native Speakers of English to accompany
THE ART OF PUBLIC SPEAKING
Stephen E. Lucas

Published by McGraw-Hill, an imprint of the McGraw-Hill Companies, Inc., 1221 Avenue of the Americas, New York, NY 10020. Copyright © 2001, 1998, 1995, 1992, 1989, 1986, 1983 by Stephen E. Lucas. All rights reserved.

The contents, or parts thereof, may be reproduced in print form solely for classroom use with the Handbook for Teachers of Non-Native Speakers of English provided such reproductions bear copyright notice, but may not be reproduced in any other form or for any other purpose without the prior written consent of the McGraw-Hill Companies, Inc., including, but not limited to, in any network or other electronic storage or transmission, or broadcast for distance learning.

5 6 7 8 9 0 QSR/QSR 0 9 8 7 6 5 4 3 2 1

ISBN 0-07-039032-0

www.mhhe.com

TABLE OF CONTENTS

Preface v
About the Authors.. vi

Part One: ESL Students and the Public Speaking Course
Introduction... 1
ESL Students' English Language Proficiency 2
ESL Students' Communicative Styles 4
ESL Students' Communication Strategies 6
Helping ESL Students Adjust to the American Classroom 8
Common Pronunciation Problems in English 11
General Descriptions of Common Native Languages.. 11
Typical Problems with the Pronunciation of Consonants by Native Languages......... 13

Part Two: Classroom Activities for ESL Students
Introduction... 15
Activity 1: ESL Student Background Questionnaire 15
Activity 2: Class Questionnaire 16
Activity 3: Recognizing Differences in Communicative Styles 17
Activity 4: Intercultural Communication Partner Activity 18
Activity 5: Communication Strategies for Effective Classroom Participation............ 19
Activity 6: Avoiding Plagiarism.. 21
Activity 7: Listening for Differences in Communication Strategies 22
Activity 8: Listening Behaviors for the Classroom.. 22
Activity 9: Phrases and Expressions for Active Listening... 23
Activity 10: Incorporating Prior Experiences into Speeches 24
Activity 11: Analyzing Sources for Speeches 24
Activity 12: Audience Analysis Interview 25
Activity 13: Using Popular Periodicals to Illustrate Viewpoints 26
Activity 14: Using Television to Illustrate Viewpoints 26
Activity 15: Advertisements and Cultural Assumptions.. 27
Activity 16: Exploring Cultural Assumptions 27
Activity 17: Audience Analysis and Adaptation Worksheet 27
Activity 18: Adapting Delivery to the Classroom Audience 28
Activity 19: Assessing Main Points 28
Activity 20: Assessing Supporting Materials 29
Activity 21: Assessing Persuasive Arguments 29
Activity 22: Analyzing Counterarguments... 30
Activity 23: Phrases and Expressions Used When Supporting Ideas 30
Activity 24: Using Connectives.. 31
Activity 25: Understanding Signposts.. 32
Activity 26: Assessing Introductions and Conclusions.. 33
Activity 27: Drafting Introductions and Conclusions 33
Activity 28: Monitoring Language Use.. 34
Activity 29: Self-assessment of Pronunciation and Grammatical Problems 34

Activity 30: Speaking Spontaneously and Maintaining Eye Contact 35
Activity 31: Facial Expressions and Gestures 36
Activity 32: Nonverbal Gestures 36
Activity 33: Individual Delivery Practice Techniques 37
Activity 34: Group Delivery Practice 37
Activity 35: Videotaped Delivery Practice 37
Activity 36: Delivery Practice with Visual Aids 38
Activity 37: Phrases and Expressions Used When Taking Turns 38
Activity 38: Phrases and Expressions Used When Exchanging Opinions 39
Activity 39: Phrases and Expressions Used When Leading a Discussion 41

Part Three: Supplemental Resources
Resources for ESL Students 42
Resources for Instructors 43
Campus Resources 45
Endnotes 45

Preface

This handbook is designed to accompany the *Instructor's Manual* to *The Art of Public Speaking* by Stephen E. Lucas. It is intended primarily for instructors who have English as a second language (ESL) students enrolled in their public speaking courses. This handbook has two major goals. The first is to help instructors become more knowledgeable about the unique strengths and weaknesses of their ESL students and to be better able to instruct them in such a way that they are able to get the most out of their experiences in a public speaking course. The second is for all students to recognize the role that culture plays in the communication process and to foster a broader understanding of intercultural communication among students in a public speaking course.

Unlike the *Instructor's Manual*, this handbook does not cover every chapter in *The Art of Public Speaking*. Instead, it begins with an overview of how instructors can become more knowledgeable about and feel more comfortable working with ESL students. It then provides classroom activities that are specifically designed for ESL students enrolled in a public speaking course.

Part One offers an overview of the central issues that should be considered when working with students from different cultural and linguistic backgrounds. In addition, it provides information that will help instructors become aware of differences in the ways ESL students communicate, participate in, and learn from their classroom experiences. The information presented in Part One is designed to help instructors recognize differences in the communicative styles of ESL students and be able to create opportunities for their ESL students to participate successfully in a public speaking course.

Part Two contains classroom activities that are appropriate for ESL students enrolled in a public speaking course. Presented in conjunction with *The Art of Public Speaking*, the activities are designed to supplement those in the *Instructor's Manual*, not to replace them. In fact, most, if not all, of the activities in the *Instructor's Manual* are appropriate for ESL students. The activities in this handbook provide instructors with additional information about the unique needs of ESL students and activities that address those needs.

As you read through this handbook you will notice that many of the activities are specifically designed for ESL students, while others are appropriate for all students enrolled in your course. You will need to decide the extent to which your ESL students need additional instructional support and which activities are most appropriate for them. In the process, we hope you will come to view your ESL students as a valuable resource in your public speaking course and that their presence there will enrich your instruction and the experiences of all your students.

Karen E. Johnson
Paula Golombek

About the Authors

Karen E. Johnson is Associate Professor of speech communication at The Pennsylvania State University. She specializes in teaching English to speakers of other languages. Her research focuses on teacher cognition in language education and the dynamics of communication in second language classrooms. She is the author of *Understanding Communication in Second Language Classrooms* (Cambridge University Press) and has published articles in *TESOL Quarterly, Teaching and Teacher Education,* and *The Journal of Reading Behavior*.

Paula Golombek is a doctoral student in the Department of Speech Communication at The Pennsylvania State University where she teaches ESL courses in the Center for English as a Second Language. Her dissertation focuses on the impact of second language teachers' personal practical knowledge on their instructional practices. She has published an article in *TESOL Quarterly*.

Part One

ESL STUDENTS AND THE PUBLIC SPEAKING COURSE

Introduction

ESL students enroll in U.S. colleges and universities for a variety of reasons. Some have lived in the U.S. for a considerable period of time, even attending U.S. high schools, and are simply pursuing higher education as are other American students. Others come to the U.S. for advanced degrees fully intending to return to their native countries to live and work. Their motivations range from a strong interest in particular majors to an urge to experience the excitement of living abroad. ESL students also enroll in public speaking courses for a variety of reasons. Some do so to fulfill graduation requirements, while others want to improve their presentational speaking skills.

Besides having different reasons for enrolling in your public speaking course, your ESL students will have tremendous variation in their English language skills. Most ESL students receive intensive study in English grammar and reading comprehension in order to pass entrance examinations for universities in their native countries. These students may do well on written exams but find face-to-face oral communication very difficult. Others have more access to U.S. television and movies and more contact with English speaking people and therefore have strong oral communication skills but weak reading and writing skills. These students may feel comfortable speaking English in social settings but struggle with the academic language required in their fields of study.

Many ESL students also struggle with nonverbal aspects of spoken communication, including eye contact, personal space, touching, and gestures. Because there are appropriate and inappropriate nonverbal behaviors in every culture, ESL students may use nonverbal behaviors that are appropriate in their native culture but inappropriate in the U.S. For example, some ESL students avoid direct eye contact with their instructors because it is considered disrespectful in their own cultures. Instructors in the U.S., however, may find lack of eye contact irritating or may incorrectly assume that their ESL students are untrustworthy or disinterested.

Many ESL students have weak listening comprehension skills. Obviously, problems can occur if a speaker's rate of speech is too fast; however, use of slang or idioms can also hinder listening comprehension. Weak listening comprehension skills can result in inappropriate verbal responses, or no response at all. Weak listening skills may also be misinterpreted as a lack of intelligence.

Finally, the English language is situated within the North American culture, and that culture influences the meanings attached to words and phrases. For example, the phrase "paper or plastic?" derives its meaning from the context in which it is used, the check-out line in a grocery store. Many ESL students lack the cultural references necessary to understand such phrases. They may have little or no functional knowledge of slang or idioms. Their choice of words may seem awkward to a native speaker. They may not be able to vary their speaking style in response to different social contexts.

In sum, speaking English as a second language involves not only acquiring new verbal and nonverbal patterns, but accepting the communication styles and speaking conventions of a new culture. A basic understanding of the unique challenges that ESL students face may give instructors a greater sensitivity to both the talents and difficulties that their ESL students bring to the public speaking course.

ESL Students' English Language Proficiency

There is a common misconception that the sole reason some ESL students do poorly in the U.S. educational system is because of their limited English language proficiency. In some cases, inadequate English skills do limit the ability of ESL students to perform well in school. But despite these limitations, all ESL students can perform at a high level if there is a supportive instructional environment in the classroom. Limited English proficiency is not and should not be seen as an insurmountable barrier to learning.

It is also important to realize that the linguistic competencies of ESL students will vary. Some students will have very strong oral communication skills, while others will be able to write grammatically correct essays. The extent of such competencies will depend on the students' prior experience with English and the contexts within which they learned English and use it daily. For example, if your ESL students learned English in their native countries primarily through rote memorization and grammar instruction, they will probably have a great deal of knowledge about the language but be less skilled at using the language to communicate. On the other hand, if your ESL students learned English through informal interactions with friends and schoolmates, they may be able to express themselves with relative ease but struggle with both reading and writing in English.

The most frequently asked question regarding ESL students in a public speaking course is "Can ESL students with heavy accents still get an A or a B in the course?" In order to answer this question, some background information on the components of spoken language is necessary.

Effective spoken language is comprised of pronunciation, fluency, and comprehensibility. Pronunciation consists of several elements. First, every language has its own phonemes, or sets of distinctive sounds, to express meaning. Some sounds that exist in one language do not exist in another. For example, the "th" sound in words like "the" and "thin" are common in English but exist in very few other languages. After puberty, it is difficult, though not impossible, for speakers to reproduce new sounds from other languages with the same proficiency as native speakers of those languages.

Spoken language also consists of proper stress and intonation patterns. In English, stress can occur on a syllable, a word, or a part of a sentence. Intonation, or rising and falling pitch changes, also occurs in words, phrases, and sentences. Stress and intonation patterns work together to give the English language a unique rhythm. Since different languages have different rhythms, ESL students whose spoken English sounds musical, staccato, or monotone are probably transferring the stress and intonation patterns from their first language to English.

Spoken language also consists of fluency, or the rate and pausing of speech. The fluency of some ESL students may sound choppy or halting to native English speakers. Others may speak too quickly, while some will speak as smoothly and as effortlessly as a native English speaker.

In addition, spoken language consists of comprehensibility, a holistic term that includes the speakers' pronunciation and fluency, as well as choice of vocabulary and grammatical control. ESL students' comprehensibility will indicate how well they are understood by native-speaking listeners. It is important to note that ESL students can have nonnative-like spoken English and still be comprehensible. It may be that they simply have a strong accent.

Given the complexity of spoken language, therefore, it may be unrealistic to expect ESL students to speak English like a native speaker. Moreover, many ESL students will feel a great deal of anxiety when speaking English, especially in the public speaking classroom, because they know their English is not native-like. When grading ESL students, you may be tempted to penalize them for their nonnative-like English. Yet some students can be comprehensible even though they may mispronounce certain sounds, have nonnative-like stress and intonation, and/or have a nonnative-like rate of speech. When you grade your ESL students, do not focus solely on their pronunciation and fluency but also on their message. Some ESL students may be capable of earning an A or a B in your course despite occasional pronunciation and fluency errors because their message is comprehensible. However, there may be other ESL students who have oral language problems that interfere with the intelligibility of their message and therefore cannot receive an above average grade.

To help make your ESL students feel more comfortable in your classroom despite their oral language problems, you may wish to meet with those ESL students whose spoken English influences their comprehensibility and hence, may negatively affect their grade. You can politely tell them that their spoken English is difficult to understand. Be as specific as possible. For example, you might tell them that they speak too quickly or that their speech sounds monotone. Find out if they have encountered situations where listeners have had difficulty understanding them. In addition, find out if they are particularly concerned about their spoken English. Remember that changing one's pronunciation can be a tremendous challenge for some ESL students. Your willingness to help your ESL students is an important first step. Tell them you may ask them to complete some of the activities in the handbook as part of the course. In addition, encourage them to seek out ESL professionals at your institution who can help them improve their spoken English.

In sum, spoken language difficulties do not have to inhibit ESL students from participating in your public speaking course; nor should they result in lower grades for ESL students. If you recognize your ESL students' oral language abilities and their needs as students, you will be better able to find ways to encourage them to participate in your public speaking course.

ESL Students' Communicative Styles

People learn to use language to communicate within a range of social and cultural contexts. This ability, generally referred to as one's communicative style, reflects the way language is used and understood within a particular culture. Moreover, it reflects and reinforces the beliefs held by members of that culture about human nature and the nature of interpersonal communication. Consider, for example, the communicative style of the Japanese, which is typically characterized as being indirect, context dependent, rich in connotation, and reflecting a responsibility to hold the interests of the group above those of the individual. In addition, the Japanese place high value on silence as opposed to explicit verbal expression, on what is perceived as socially acceptable over individual feelings, and on an overwhelming need not to offend. Now consider the experience of a Japanese student in a U.S. college classroom in which individual ideas are given priority and in which the speaker, not the listener, is responsible for making one's self understood. Such differences in communicative styles tend to create stereotypes of the Japanese as reticent and indirect and of Americans as outspoken and pushy.

Besides such obvious differences, communicative styles can differ in more subtle ways. In the Mexican-American community, for example, children tend to work collectively and cooperatively with others, which in turn produces a good deal of turn-taking, negotiation of shared responsibility, and collaboration in the completion of tasks. While Mexican-American children are sometimes expected to demonstrate their ability to lead by assuming a more competitive role, they are more often encouraged to cooperate in collaborative ways with others. Consequently, in U.S. schools Mexican-American students are often found by their teachers to resist working individually and to share their answers with others. This, of course, violates their U.S. teachers' belief in the importance of individual work. In addition, although Mexican-American parents expect their children to obey and to respect parental authority, they simultaneously provide their children the freedom to decide how a task will be accomplished. In contrast, U.S. teachers tend to control all aspects of an assignment, allowing students little, if any, opportunity to negotiate their role in how the assignment will be completed. Thus while Mexican-American students tend to possess competencies in collaboration, cooperation, and independent decision making, their communicative styles are often discouraged in American schools.[1]

Simply observing your ESL students can tell you a great deal about what they know and do not know about how to act and interact in a U.S. classroom. Make a point of observing your ESL students during the first few weeks of class. Try to observe what they do and say in a variety of social and instructional contexts. Ask yourself the following questions:

1. Does the student ever volunteer answers to your questions?

2. Does the student tend to answer questions that ask for factual or opinion answers?

3. Does the student respond and seem comfortable when called on?

4. Does the student participate and seem comfortable working in small groups?

5. Does the student participate and seem comfortable working in pairs?

6. Does the student seek you out before class? After class? During office hours?

7. Does the student ask questions about assignments?

8. Do you notice any other characteristics of the student's communicative behavior?

Some ESL students come from cultures in which the status of the instructor and the role of students are very different from what is found in the typical U.S. classroom. For example, a Taiwanese student described her experience as a student in Taiwan and the difficulty she experienced adjusting to her studies at a U.S. university:

> When I first came here, I couldn't believe how much Americans talked in class. In Taiwan, students never speak in class unless the teacher calls on them. At first, I was afraid to talk in class because I thought I might ask a question that I should know the answer, or I might say something that was already said. I was afraid that what was interesting to me might not be interesting to the rest of the students. I kept waiting for my teachers to call on me, but they never did. Then I realized that this way of talking was what teachers expected, and so I would have to get used to it. I think I have talked more in my classes here than all my years of schooling in Taiwan.[2]

This student characterized her Taiwanese teachers as having a lecture style of teaching and reported that students were expected to be silent. Little, if any, class discussion occurred, and it was considered rude for a student to interrupt the teacher to ask a question. This student's perceptions of appropriate classroom behavior were based on her culturally acquired ways of interacting, which included a reluctance to draw attention to one's self and a tendency to hold the needs of the group over those of the individual.

Finding out about your ESL students' prior experiences and preconceived notions about appropriate classroom behavior can give you a great deal of insight into who your ESL students are and why they interact the way they do in your classroom. Make a point of opening the lines of communication with your ESL students early in the course. Find out about their prior experiences in U.S. classrooms, if they went to high school in the U.S., or if your class is one of their first U.S. classroom experiences. Encourage them to express their ideas about what they believe is and is not appropriate language and behavior in the classroom.

In addition, you might schedule an individual meeting with each of your ESL students early in the course. This should be done during your office hours when you both have time to talk and will not be interrupted. Questions that might help you better understand your ESL students include:

1. Did you attend junior or senior high school in the United States?

2. How are students expected to talk and act in classrooms in your country?

3. How are teachers perceived in classrooms in your country?

4. When is it appropriate for students to ask questions in class in your country?

5. If you were unsure of the material in class covered in class in your country, what would you do?

6. What do you find to be the major differences between classrooms in your country and in the United States?

Take this interview as an opportunity to explain what is and is not considered appropriate communicative language and behavior in your public speaking course. Some ESL students, for example, will tell you that they feel uncomfortable asking questions in class, since in their own cultures asking a question might be viewed as a challenge to the teacher's authority. Explain that most American instructors welcome questions from students and, in fact, see questions as a way to judge whether or not students understand the content of the lesson. Look for similar opportunities throughout the interview to describe your expectations for communication in your classroom.

ESL Students' Communication Strategies

Just as communicative styles differ from one culture to another, so do the ways information is organized in oral and written communication. As an instructor, you may notice speeches by your ESL students that seem a bit "out of focus" or "lacking organization." Such tendencies may be related to culturally specific rhetorical strategies of oral and written communication.

For example, one analysis of the rhetorical organization of essays written by Arab, Asian, Spanish, French, and Russian speakers in an ESL composition class found that the organizational strategies of these students' essays varied widely from those of typical native-English speakers.[3] The Arab students tended to organize their essays using a series of parallel constructions in which all the ideas were coordinately linked and contained very little subordination. The essays read like a series of seemingly unrelated ideas that were never explicitly connected one to another. On the other hand, the Asian students tended to organize their essays in a circular fashion, often indirectly addressing the central issue by developing it in terms of what it is not, as opposed to what it is. The point of their essays was often unclear to U.S. instructors. The French, Spanish, and Russian students tended to organize their essays in a series of parallel constructions that contained a number of subordinate structures, thereby creating digressions from the main idea of the essay. Each of these organizational strategies was found to differ from the linear nature of the typical English essay with its topic statement, series of subdivisions of that topic statement supported by examples and illustrations, and development of a central idea relating to all other ideas in the essay.

This is not to say that any organizational strategy is superior to another, only that there are differences. If an audience expects an essay or a speech to be organized in a linear fashion, any of the alternative organizational strategies mentioned above may create confusion or misinterpretation of the speaker's ideas. As with other differences in the communication strategies of ESL students, culturally specific rhetorical strategies of organization must be recognized. If your ESL students give speeches that never seem to get to the point or that consistently diverge from the main point, it may be that the students are relying on patterns of speech organization specific to their native language and culture. Since this will affect how they are perceived by U.S. listeners, you will need to spend time helping your ESL students recognize the rhetorical strategies associated with different types of speeches and provide opportunities for them to adjust their oral presentations to the organizational strategies expected by U.S. listeners and instructors.

Another way to understand differences in culturally specific rhetorical strategies is through anthropologist Edward T. Hall's definition of high-context and low-context cultures.[4] Hall defines a high-context culture as one in which most of the information in an interaction between people is either embedded in the physical context or is internalized in those people. In other words, very little information is coded in the verbal message. Because so much information is embedded in the context, it is not necessary to state the obvious. On the other hand, in low-context cultures very little information is embedded in the context or the people in the interaction. Most of the information is coded in the verbal message and is much more explicit. Hall views cultures along a continuum with high-context and low-context cultures on either end of the continuum. Examples of high-context cultures include Japan, Korea, and Taiwan, whereas examples of low-context cultures include Germany, Scandinavia, and the United States.

Because Hall argues that the level of context influences a culture's language and communicative behavior, we can view rhetorical structures as being culturally influenced. As a result, if you have students from different cultures, they may rely on different rhetorical structures to express themselves. In practical terms, preview statements in the introduction of a speech, connectives throughout the body, and summaries of the main points in the conclusion are appropriate in the U.S. and other low-context cultures. In a high-context culture, however, such devices may make a speaker appear to be stating the obvious or to be insulting the audience.

As the instructor in a public speaking course, it is essential for you to recognize that in most cases the communication strategies of your ESL students will differ from the communication strategies of your U.S. students. Moreover, these differences, whether obvious or subtle, can inhibit the ability of ESL students to participate fully in and to learn from your classroom instruction. In addition, it is essential to recognize that these differences in communication strategies are not caused by any sort of deficiency among ESL students but reflect different cultural backgrounds and contexts. You can help your ESL students succeed in your public speaking course by recognizing the differences in their communication strategies and by assisting them in adjusting to the communication strategies of the U.S. college classroom.

Helping ESL Students Adjust to the U.S. Classroom

If you want your ESL students to succeed in your public speaking course, you must begin where they are and gradually bring them to where they can communicate effectively. This means devising ways to take advantage of the communicative competencies they already possess and then helping them acquire, or at least adjust to, aspects of the communicative language and behavior they need to succeed in your class. For example, if after getting to know your ESL students it becomes apparent that they are comfortable answering factual questions but feel uneasy about offering their opinions, tailor the nature of your questions accordingly. On the other hand, if you find that your ESL students feel extremely uncomfortable volunteering in class but are willing to offer an answer when called on, adjust your behavior accordingly. If your ESL students seem more comfortable speaking in small groups than in front of the entire class, arrange your lessons to include some small-group activities. In general, consider ways you can adjust your teaching to take advantage of your ESL students' communicative competencies.

It is also important to recognize that ESL students may have different learning styles. Some are strong visual learners, others prefer listening and taking notes, while still others prefer manipulating actual objects or interacting with other people. Since you may have ESL students from an array of cultures, vary the modes through which you present information, as well as the modes through which you expect students to learn.

Your ESL students may have difficulty speaking and listening in English. If they seem to have difficulty understanding you, consider adapting your communicative language and behavior in the following ways:

1. Watch ESL students for feedback as to whether or not they understand what you are saying.

2. Allow ESL students enough time to respond. Listen for feedback. Don't put words in their mouths because you are growing impatient.

3. Watch your use of idioms and slang. Many ESL students are not familiar with informal expressions used in the U.S. If you use idioms or slang, explain the phrases you have used.

4. If your ESL students do not appear to understand you, don't say the same thing again in a louder voice. Try to speak more slowly. Or paraphrase your ideas.

5. Be careful of words with multiple meanings. For example, ESL speakers may know the word "funny" in the sense of comical, but not as awkward.

6. Be aware of your references to popular culture. ESL students may not be familiar with these.

7. Use comprehension checks such as "Do you understand?"

8. Use clarification requests when you are not sure what an ESL student has said. Such requests include "I think what you mean . . ." or "So, what you are saying is . . ."

9. Ask ESL students to repeat things in their own words to see if they understand.

10. Most important, do not be condescending to your ESL students. They are not stupid; they are just not native speakers of English.

All students, whether ESL or native speakers of English, will take their cues for how to participate in class from what you do and say. If you accept students' answers as valid contributions to your class discussions, even if those answers are not exactly what you were looking for, students will quickly recognize that there is more than one right answer to any given question and that what they say will be respected. If, on the other hand, you accept only the answer you are looking for, students will be more reticent to offer their comments for fear of being wrong. In some cultures, being wrong in a public forum is threatening. Many ESL students report that they would rather remain silent than risk making a mistake in front of a class. In addition, what you may perceive as a minor correction ("Well, that's not exactly what I was looking for . . . does anyone else know the answer?") may be perceived by ESL students as a severe criticism.

You can also help your ESL students adjust to the communicative behavior expected in U.S. classrooms by making your instructional activities predictable. When students know exactly what is expected of them and have ample opportunity to prepare, they are more willing and able to participate. To do this, you need to show, as opposed to merely telling, your students what is expected of them. Consider, for example, that you are helping students prepare for their informative speeches. You might start the unit by showing a sample informative speech videotape as a model and then by using that model to help the class generate the critical components of an effective informative speech. You might also use the model to help students generate topics for their speeches. Showing students what you expect them to do can be of great help for ESL students.

Making your instructional activities predictable also means giving students ample opportunity to prepare for what you expect them to say and do. This means providing opportunities for your students to test out and/or rehearse their ideas in private or in small groups before performing in front of the class. For example, instead of asking students to read a chapter and be ready to discuss it during the next class, you might provide two or three specific questions that you want them to pay attention to when reading and then start the discussion by asking those questions. Or you might begin class by asking small groups of students to generate questions or comments that they have about the chapter and then by having each group present one question or comment to the class for discussion. Since ESL students are often reluctant to speak in class, giving them an opportunity to formulate and rehearse their ideas before making those ideas public will minimize the risk they may experience when trying to participate in class.

In addition to recognizing differences in your students' communicative styles, you might also want to analyze the communicative demands of the activities that you use during classroom instruction. This means identifying how your students are expected to participate in any given activity. Imagine, for example, that you are leading a class discussion of the review questions at the end of a chapter in *The Art of Public Speaking.* You want to see if your students understand the information in the chapter, and you want to give them an opportunity to ask questions. Typically, you might ask the first review question and wait for a volunteer. If no one volunteers, you might call on a student. Once you get a response, you might try to tie the student's answer to an issue covered in the chapter. At some point, you might pose an open-ended question in which you ask other students to contribute to the discussion. Your aim is to generate a lively discussion with participation from most of the students in the class.

For your ESL students to participate in this kind of class discussion, they need to know when it is and is not appropriate for them to speak. This may require knowing whether or not they need to wait to be called on, or if they are expected to volunteer an answer on their own. They may need to know how to take and, at times, hold the floor. They may also need to know when it is appropriate to offer factual versus opinion-based answers. They may even need to know how to disagree politely with you or their classmates. If you notice your ESL students having difficulty participating in an activity, it may suggest that they need to learn how to adjust to the communicative demands of your instruction and the U.S. classroom.

Make your ESL students aware of a range of compensation strategies that they can use when making speeches. Stress to them that a clearly organized speech is one way to compensate for limited English proficiency. Clear and effective introductions and conclusions as discussed in the textbook and in class are also helpful. The use of connectives can aid listeners by helping them follow the organization. It is also important for ESL students to be audience-centered when preparing and delivering their speeches. If the speaker makes an attempt to appeal directly to his or her audience, the audience may respond by listening harder to the speaker. In addition, encourage ESL students to carefully articulate important words that are repeated throughout a speech, to practice articulating words with which they have problems, and to reinforce their spoken language through written language or visual aids.

Another way to help ESL students adjust to the U.S. classroom is to use small groups as part of your classroom instruction. Speaking in small groups enables ESL students to take a more active role in what they are learning, as well as to have more opportunities to contribute to and to help formulate the information that is generated and learned in class.

More often than not, the extent to which ESL students are willing to participate in and contribute to small group activities depends on how they think their contributions will be received. To some extent, these perceptions are linked to the perceived status and/or abilities of individual group members. For example, if a student is perceived by his or her peers as more competent, group members may well defer to that student, thereby limiting their own opportunities for interaction and influence in the group. However, instructors can bolster ESL students' feelings of competence by consistently accepting their contributions in class discussions and by showing that they value those contributions. This does not imply that you should accept everything your ESL students offer, but that you should seek to foster their sense of competence by encouraging them to make connections between what they already know and what they are learning in your course.

In Part Two of this handbook, you will find a wide range of activities from which you can select to help meet the special instructional needs of your ESL students. The last three sections of Part One explain some of the most common pronunciation patterns and errors of non-native speakers of English.

Common Pronunciation Problems In English

For most nonnative speakers, the differences between the following vowels are difficult to hear and produce:

/ i / and / I /	("he" and "hit")
/ æ / and / ∈ /	("mad" and "met")
/ a / and / ɔ /	("lay" and "law")
/ uw / and / ∩ /	("too" and "took")

Inflectional endings such as -s, -es, -d, and -ed, as well as -teen and -ty on numbers, are difficult to hear and pronounce. For most speakers this is truly a pronunciation problem and not a grammar problem. For others, it is a question of both grammar and pronunciation.

Consonant clusters are difficult for most nonnative speakers, who tend to leave out sounds or to add vowel sounds between the consonants in the cluster. For example:

Put the (des**ks** / des:s) in the corner.
He had (adap**ted** / adapt) well to this country.
John (wal**ks** / walk) to work each morning.
We (**fl**ew / few) in to town yesterday.

The stress, rhythm, and intonation patterns of English can also be difficult for nonnative speakers to master. A stressed or accented syllable is one that is more prominent than the other syllables in a word. Stress is marked by length, pitch, and loudness. In English, stress can fall on almost any syllable of a word. In many other languages, stress regularly falls on the same syllable; therefore, nonnative speakers may have difficulty changing the location of stress on certain English words. Note, for example, the different stress on the following words: ph<u>o</u>tograph; phot<u>o</u>graphy; photog<u>ra</u>phic.

Rhythm is closely connected to stressed and unstressed syllables. In unstressed syllables, vowels are reduced. In stressed syllables, vowels are longer and are spoken with more volume. Intonation has to do with the rise and fall of the pitch level.

English has specific intonation patterns for final rising-falling as used in statements; for commands, yes-no and information questions; and for non-final rising as used in lists. Nonnative speakers must be sure that their intonation falls and rises enough or, for example, a statement may be misinterpreted as a question.

General Descriptions of Common Native Languages

Arabic

There are several dialects of Arabic (for example, Egyptian Arabic, Iraqi Arabic, Moroccan Arabic). Arabic is a stress-timed language in which unstressed vowels are not reduced to the extent that they are in English. However, word stress in Arabic is fairly regular relative to English word stress.

Chinese

Although Mandarin is the national language, the dialects spoken by people from different regions can cause different problems for spoken English. In addition, there are variations among Chinese people from Hong Kong, the People's Republic of China, Taiwan, and Singapore. The Chinese languages or dialects are tonal. Mandarin, for example, has four tones, whereas Cantonese has nine. In addition, Chinese uses characters rather than letters in an alphabet, so it does not have sounds that coordinate with letters. Rather, the same characters can have different meanings depending on the tone that is used. The Chinese often learn British English, which may be reflected in their pronunciation, word choice, and syllable stress.

Hindi

Indian English is a dialect, and many Indians speak it fluently and consider themselves fluent in English. Yet some native speakers of English in the United States perceive Indian English to be accented or less than fluent. Thus it can be insulting to some Indians when their English-speaking ability is questioned. Because Indians have many native languages, including Hindi, Bengali, Urdu, and Tamil, it is quite complex to detail the unique differences of each language. In several, however, the intonation of Indian dialects rises and falls to much higher and lower levels than the intonation of standard American English. In addition, Indians who speak English usually learn British English, whose pronunciation, word choice, and syllable stress is often different from that of American English.

Japanese

Japanese is referred to as a pitch-accent language. This means that Japanese speakers use a mora rather than a syllable. A mora is a unit of time; each mora takes about the same length of time to say (the most common type of mora is a consonant followed by a vowel). A mora may be differentiated by pitch, rather than by intensity, as is the case with syllable stress in English. Thus Japanese speakers of English may sound as though they are giving equal stress to all syllables in a word or to all words in a sentence.

Korean

Korean is the only language used in Korea, although there are dialects spoken in different geographical regions. In Korean, one character stands for one syllable, making the Korean language sound harder, clearer, and less rhythmic than English. The rate of speech in Korean is about a third slower than the rate of speech in English.

Russian

The most distinguishing feature of Russian is the presence of hard and soft consonants. Most consonants can be either hard or soft depending on the kind of vowel that follows them. All vowels are paired according to their hard or soft qualities. Russian does not have fixed stress. The stress may fall on any part of the word and even shift in different grammatical forms of a single word.

Spanish

Spanish word stress is quite regular, with most words being stressed on the second-to-last syllable. However, Spanish does use variation in stress to differentiate words of different meanings. Irregular stress is marked with an accent marker. Spanish speakers' pronunciation of English words and sentences may lack the vowel reduction necessary for English rhythm.

Typical Problems With the Pronunciation of Consonants by Native Language

The following chart simplifies the articulatory processes that nonnative speakers of English use when speaking English.[5] It is important to note that this chart is not intended to stereotype speakers of any language or to be comprehensive. Although these are some common ways that ESL students pronounce different English sounds, not all speakers of a given language make these articulations, and some speakers will have other difficulties. Instructors should ask their ESL students about their pronunciation difficulties and should note themselves the patterns they hear in their students' speech.

Arabic	Pronounce:	/ p / like / b / "pet" sounds like "bet"
	Roll:	/ r / "rim" sounds like "rrim"
	Substitute:	/ t / for / Φ / "three" sounds like "tree"
		/ d / for / ð / "those" sounds like "dose"
Chinese	Do not distinguish:	/ p / and / b / in final position "cap" and "cab" may sound identical
		/ l / and / n / in initial position "light" and "night" may sound identical
	Pronounce:	/ l / like / w / "mole" sounds like "mow"
		/ y / in initial position "east" sounds like "yeast"
	Substitute:	/ t / or / f / for / Φ / "three" sounds like "tree" "with" sounds like "wif"

Hindi	Pronounce:	/ v / like / b / "very" sounds like "berry"
		/ f / like / p / "fan" sounds like "pan"
		/ w / like / v / "wine" sounds like "vine"
Japanese	Do not distinguish:	/ r / and / l / "right" sounds like "light"
	Substitute:	/ v / for / b / "boat" sounds like "vote"
Korean	Pronounce:	/ s / like / sh / "see" sounds like "she"
		/ z / like / d / "zen" sounds like "den"
		/ r / like / l / "right" sounds like "light"
	Substitute:	/ v / for / b / "boat" sounds like "vote"
		/ p / for / f / "fan" sounds like "pan"
Russian	Pronounce:	/ v / like / w / "vail" sounds like "wail"
		/ Φ / like / s / or / z / "these" sounds like "seese" or "zeese"
	Roll:	/ r / "rain" sounds like "rrain"
Spanish	Substitute:	/ v / for / b / "boat" sounds like "vote"
		/ tr / for / r / "ship" sounds like "chip"
		/ s / like / z / "zone" sounds like "sone?
		/ dz / for / y / "use" sounds like "juice"

/ t / for / Φ /
"three" sounds like "tree"

/ d / for / ð /
"those" sounds like "dose"

Roll: / r /
"rim" sounds like "rrim"

Part Two

CLASSROOM ACTIVITIES FOR ESL STUDENTS

Introduction

Part Two of this handbook contains classroom activities that are appropriate for ESL students in a public speaking course. The activities can be completed individually or in small groups depending on the number of ESL students you have and their specific oral language abilities. Some of the activities focus on information presented in *The Art of Public Speaking,* while others focus on general matters that are appropriate for ESL students in a public speaking course. The titles of the activities should help you select those most appropriate for your ESL students. Finally, the activities are sequenced to follow the order of the chapters in *The Art of Public Speaking.* The particular sequence you follow, of course, will depend on the needs of your ESL students.

Activity 1:

ESL Student Background Questionnaire

On the first day of class, have your ESL students fill out and return the following questionnaire. This will give you an idea of their language backgrounds and prior public speaking experiences.

Name: _____

1.   What country are you from?

2.   What is your native language?

3. How long have you studied English? In what contexts?

4. How would you rate your spoken English?

5. How long have you been in the United States?

6. Have you ever taken a public speaking course? If so, describe the course.

7. Have you ever had an opportunity to speak in public? If so, describe the speech(es) you gave.

8. Why have you enrolled in this public speaking course?

9. What do you hope to learn from this public speaking course?

Activity 2:

Class Questionnaire

Have the entire class fill out and return the following questionnaire. Follow up with a discussion of the students' responses. This will give you an idea of the range of your students' language backgrounds and experiences with people from other cultures.

1. Have you studied a foreign language? If yes, which language(s), for how long, and in what context?

2. Have you ever studied or traveled abroad? If yes, explain.

3. Do you plan to study, travel, or work abroad in the future? If yes, explain.

4. Do you have any friends from other cultures? If yes, describe them briefly and explain how you know them.

5. Have you had teachers from other cultures? If yes, explain.

6. Do you recall an experience with a nonnative speaker of English in which you had difficulty making yourself understood? If yes, describe the experience and why you think the miscommunication occurred.

7. Do you recall an experience in which you had difficulty understanding a nonnative speaker of English? If yes, describe the experience and why you think the miscommunication occurred.

Activity 3:

Recognizing Differences in Communicative Styles

This exercise gives your students an opportunity to role-play different communicative styles in class. Divide the class into groups of two students each. Pass out the appropriate instructions (see below), telling the students in each group not to share their instructions with each other. Give students several minutes to read the instructions and then ask the students in each group to talk with one another for five minutes.

At the end of the time limit, come together as a class. Ask one member of each group to describe the communicative style of his or her partner. Ask the other member to do the same. Write the descriptions on the board. After this, ask the class to comment on how differences in communicative styles might affect communication with persons from other cultures.

Instructions for Partner A

When speaking with your partner, do the following:

1. Try to make eye contact with your partner as often as possible. In your culture, people who do not look you in the eye seem to have something to hide or else they seem extremely uncomfortable and awkward.

2. Speak in a loud, clear voice. This is valued in your culture because it shows friendliness. A person who speaks quietly is seen as awkward.

3. Use a lot of hand gestures. This gives a feeling of casualness.

4. Stand close to the person you are talking to. Touching a person is considered a gesture of sincerity and friendship in your culture.

5. If there is silence, try to fill it with conversation. Your culture does not feel comfortable with silence.

6. Do not ask personal questions. In your culture, when you meet someone for the first time, you talk only about superficial topics. Topics that are appropriate for an initial contact include the weather, where you are from, what you do, etc. You do not want to get too personal at this point.

Instructions for Partner B

When speaking with your partner, do the following:

1. Try not to make eye contact with your partner. It is rude in your culture to look someone in the eye. To show respect, you look down when you are talking with someone.

2. Speak in a soft voice. Your culture values people who speak softly, although not so softly that you are unable to hear them.

3. Do not use hand gestures. In your culture, hand gestures are believed to call attention to a person, and you don't want to stand out.

4. Try to stand or sit at least three feet away from your partner. In your culture a person would not stand or sit close to or touch anyone but a spouse or a very close friend.

5. If there is silence, do not try to fill it with conversation. Your culture believes that silence conveys a message and allows you to appreciate the subtle aspects of social interaction.

6. Ask very personal questions. It is extremely important in your culture to know the status of the person you are talking to so you know whether or not you should defer to that person. As a result, when you first meet someone, you want to ask questions that will tell you something about the other person's status. Appropriate questions include: What do your parents do for a living? What is your grade point average? Did your parents go to college? Where does your family vacation?

Activity 4:

Intercultural Communication Partner Activity

This exercise gives your students an opportunity to interact with a person from another culture. It is intended to help them learn about another culture and to encourage them to examine the nonverbal behavior and public speaking patterns of other cultures.

Students should conduct an interview with someone from a different culture about the nonverbal behavior and public speaking patterns of his or her culture. Questions to be asked in the interview include:

1. How much do speakers move around? Do they stand or sit?

2. Do speakers use hand gestures? What amount of gesturing is considered appropriate or inappropriate?

3. Do speakers make eye contact with audience members? Does this differ for male and female speakers?

4. How loud a voice is appropriate for public speaking? Does this differ for men and women? Is vocal variety considered appropriate?

5. Do people announce their topic at the beginning of their speech, in the middle, or at the end?

6. Is there an introduction to a speech? If so, what goes in it?

7. How do you conclude a speech?

8. Every time you make a new point, do you have to announce it to your listeners?

9. What kinds of supporting materials are appropriate? Statistics? Testimony? Examples? Religious references?

10. What kind of language is appropriate?

11. What is the most striking similarity between public speaking in your culture and in the United States? What is the most striking difference?

Students are to spend at least an hour with the person they interview. They should take notes during the interview. After the interview, give students the option to report on their interview by making a short oral presentation based on the following questions:

1. What do you feel is most different with respect to public speaking between your interviewee's culture and your own?

2. How did you adapt during the interview to the speaker's rate of speech, choice of language, choice of references, and the like?

3. How has this interview reinforced your ideas about the culture of the person you interviewed? How has this interview expanded your ideas about the culture of the person you interviewed?

Activity 5:

Communication Strategies for Effective Classroom Participation

List the following verbal expressions and nonverbal behaviors on a handout. Meet with your ESL students as a group and discuss when it is and is not appropriate to use these expressions or behaviors when participating in classroom discussions. During the meeting, encourage your ESL students to ask about and/or to describe other expressions and behaviors they may have heard or seen U.S. students use during classroom discussions. In addition, encourage them to describe differences they may notice between communication strategies in the U.S. classroom and classrooms in their own cultures.

1. Getting into the discussion

    Verbal Expressions   *Nonverbal Behaviors*

    "May I ask a question?"   Raising your hand

    "I have a question."   Leaning forward

"I'd like to know . . ."   Nodding or shaking your head

"I'd like to comment on that point . . ."   Holding up a finger

"Might I add . . ."   Nodding toward the speaker

2. Holding the floor

Hesitating   *Rephrasing*

"Well, . . ."   "In other words, you want to know . . ."

"Umm, let's see."   "So, you're asking me . . ."

"Let me think."   "So it seems that you think . . ."

3. Offering factual versus opinion-based answers

Factual Questions   *Opinion Questions*

"What does this mean?"   "What do you think this means?"

"What is the answer to number 2?"   "Do you agree or disagree with number 2?"

"What was the reading about?"   "What did you think of the reading?"

4. Agreeing and disagreeing during a discussion

Expressions of Agreement   *Expressions of Disagreement*

"Right."   "I'm not sure I agree with that."

"That's true."   "I'm sorry, but I disagree."

"I agree with what you just said."   "Your view is slightly different from mine."

"I couldn't agree more."   "That may be true, but don't you think . . . ?"

"You're absolutely right about that."   "I may be way off base, but . . ."

To reinforce these phrases and expressions, give your ESL students an optional assignment in which they observe a class (either your public speaking class or another class) and take note of the expressions that U.S. students use to participate in the discussion. You may want to hold a follow-up meeting with your ESL students in which you discuss their observations.

Another option might be to ask your ESL students to participate in a class discussion and then write a one-page paper in which they evaluate the extent to which they were able to use the expressions listed above as communication strategies to participate in the discussion. In their papers they should:

1. Describe the ways in which they participated in the discussion.

2. Describe how they felt about their ability to participate in the discussion.

3. Describe how they might have participated more in the discussion.

Activity 6:

Avoiding Plagiarism

Plagiarism is one of the most pressing ethical issues facing students in a public speaking course. Accurate documentation of sources is an important convention in both oral and written communication. In the U.S., individual opinions are highly valued and speakers and writers expect to be given credit for their ideas. In some cultures, however, the borrowing of ideas is viewed differently. Some ESL students learn to speak and write by imitating the work of great speakers or great writers and are praised for good imitations. In addition, ESL students may not feel that their English language skills are strong enough to express an author's ideas in their own words. Such students may not understand the conventions of documenting sources and may unintentionally commit plagiarism. This activity is designed to help your ESL students understand that they need to use quotations and paraphrases in ways that avoid plagiarism.

Provide your students with your university's statement on plagiarism and give some examples of plagiarism in a speech. Have students, in groups or class discussion, explain why each example is a case of plagiarism and suggest ways to correct the problem. Use the Guidelines for Avoiding Plagiarism listed below to direct your discussion. Ask students to present their ideas to the class as to what these guidelines suggest about U.S. values concerning ownership of ideas. Ask ESL students to share their culture's ideas about plagiarism and the use of sources.

Guidelines for Avoiding Plagiarism: Plagiarism is presenting someone else's ideas or language as your own. Here is how to avoid plagiarism.

1. Avoid using the exact words of a speaker or writer without making it clear that the words are being taken from another source.

2. Avoid paraphrasing a speaker's or author's words without identifying the speaker or author.

3. Avoid giving a speech written by someone else and presenting it as your own.

4. Avoid having anyone write any part of your speech for you.

5. Put things in your own words.

6. Use proper formats for citing and documenting sources.

Activity 7:

Listening for Differences in Communication Strategies

Assign your ESL students to listen to a lecture in one of their other classes. Ask them to analyze the lecture in light of the following questions:

1. Does the speaker meet your expectations in terms of the structure of the lecture? What does the speaker do most effectively? What would you suggest to improve the speaker's lecture?

2. Did you have any difficulty following the speaker? If so, is the difficulty because you had problems understanding the speaker's English or does the difficulty stem from the structure or content of the lecture? Is there anything you can do to improve your ability to keep track of the speaker's ideas?

During a follow-up meeting with your ESL students, discuss the following questions:

1. Did they notice rhetorical devices such as previewing main points in the introduction, using connectives, or avoiding language that is inappropriate for the audience?

2. Could they understand the speaker? If they could, was it due to the structure of the lecture, the speaker's language, or both? If they could not understand the speaker, was it due to structure, language, or both?

3. What can they do to increase their comprehension of the speaker's ideas?

Activity 8:

Listening Behaviors for the Classroom

This exercise is designed to help students consider whether or not interactions between native and nonnative speakers of English are the same as those that involve only native speakers of English. It should help students see similarities and differences between these two types of interactions. The discussion may also bring out students' prejudices about dealing with nonnative speakers. Some students may feel frustration or anger when dealing with nonnative speakers, especially if the speaker is a teacher or teaching assistant. On the other hand, nonnative speakers may express anxiety about speaking and listening in such interactions. If nonnative speakers do not express the reasons for their anxiety, the instructor can point out how difficult it is to communicate in another language. For example, ESL students must not only work to follow the conversation, but must also respond in an appropriate manner. They may have limited or no knowledge of slang, or they may miss ideas due to the speaker's rate of speech. Or they may take extra time to formulate a response, which may lead to impatience on the part of the native speaker.

Lead a discussion in which students develop a code of listening behavior for their classroom in combination with that described in Chapter Three of the *Instructor's Manual* for *The Art of Public Speaking*. Students should give special attention to listening behaviors for situations in which ESL students are participants. Students should consider whether there are listening behaviors that might be distinct for interactions between native speakers of English and ESL speakers. If so, students should try to identify those behaviors.

Activity 9:

Phrases and Expressions for Active Listening

Below are some useful phrases and expressions that may help your ESL students become active listeners. List them on a handout and then meet with your ESL students as a group to discuss appropriate usage. During the discussion, encourage your ESL students to ask about and/or to describe other expressions they may have heard U.S. students use. In addition, encourage the ESL students to describe differences they may have noticed between the U.S. expressions and those that are commonly used in their own cultures.

Asking for Clarification

"What do you mean?"

"I'm not sure what you mean."

"Sorry, but I don't understand."

"Could you explain what you mean by . . . ?"

Clarifying or Restating

"I mean . . ."

"In other words . . ."

"The point I'm trying to make is . . ."

"What I'm trying to say is . . ."

Paraphrasing

"What she means is . . ."

"I believe his point is . . ."

"I think she feels . . . . Isn't that right?"

Checking for Understanding

"Do you see what I mean?"

"Is that clear?"

"So, you think that . . ."

To reinforce these phrases and expressions, give your ESL students an optional assignment in which they observe a class (either your public speaking class or another class) and take note of the expressions that demonstrate active listening. You may want to hold a follow-up meeting with your ESL students in which you discuss their observations.

Another option might be to ask your ESL students to participate in a class discussion and then write a one-page paper in which they evaluate the extent to which they were active listeners. In their papers, students should:

1. Describe the ways in which they actively listened.

2. Describe how they felt about their ability to actively listen.

3. Describe how they might have been a more active listener.

Activity 10:

Incorporating Prior Experiences into Speeches

As mentioned in Part One, some ESL students may be reluctant to use their own knowledge and experience in their speeches since displays of personal expression may be considered inappropriate in their cultures. As a result, it may be useful to tell ESL students that it is appropriate to include information based on their prior experiences in their speeches.

Have ESL students create a list of topics from which they could speak based on their prior experiences. If your ESL students have difficulty coming up with topics, provide them with the following list of possible topics:

Becoming bicultural	Learning a second language
Experiencing culture shock	Communicating interculturally
Parent-child relationships	Women's rights
Dating practices	Their educational system

Ask your ESL students to describe their prior experiences with these topics and to discuss how they might fit those experiences into their speeches.

Activity 11:

Analyzing Sources for Speeches

Have your ESL students prepare an in-progress list of library sources that they are using to prepare their speeches. Have them evaluate the appropriateness of these sources by asking the following questions:

1. Are the sources too technical for this audience? Explain.

2. Are the sources biased? Explain.

3. Are the sources too informal for this audience? Explain.

Have your ESL students turn in their list of sources after they have evaluated it. Return the list with comments as to the appropriateness of the sources and suggest additional sources where necessary.

Activity 12:

Audience Analysis Interview

ESL students may have difficulty analyzing an audience in the U.S. First, because some ESL students do not interact with Americans on a regular basis, they may not know a great deal about American culture. Thus they may lack basic cultural references and have difficulty accurately analyzing the audience when preparing a speech. Second, because ESL students come from varying cultures, they may have different perceptions about American culture than their native-born classmates. It is also possible that they have stereotypes of people in the United States.

To help your ESL students with audience analysis, try supplementing the Application Exercises in Chapter 5 of the *Instructor's Manual* for *The Art of Public Speaking* with the following:

Pair each of your ESL students with a native speaker classmate and ask each to interview the other on the following topics. Each student should answer from his or her own cultural perspective. As a class, tabulate the results on the board for comparison and discussion.

Sample topics:

Gun control	Gay rights
Women's rights	Religion and politics
Gambling	Terrorism
Abortion	Illegal immigration
Nuclear energy	Affirmative action
Free speech	Legalization of drugs

Sample interview questions:

1. What do you know about this topic?

2. What is your stance on this topic? Explain why.

3. Who else might agree with your stance on this topic? Explain why.

4. Who might disagree with your stance on this topic? Explain why.

ESL students may benefit from this activity by becoming informed of different perspectives on these issues and where such perspectives come from. In addition, the activity can help all students become more aware of the cultural perspectives of their classmates. It also gives instructors concrete examples illustrating the importance of different frames of reference in the communication process.

Activity 13:

Using Popular Periodicals to Illustrate Viewpoints

This activity will help ESL students become familiar with "typical" U.S. attitudes toward controversial issues. In addition, it will help them become more aware of their own culturally-based attitudes and the role these attitudes can play in the preparation of a public speech.

Encourage ESL students to choose a controversial issue such as school choice, affirmative action, violence in the media, or welfare reform for one of their speeches. Ask them to read articles from several popular periodicals, each of which has its own perspective. For a more liberal perspective, you might suggest they read *The New Republic, Mother Jones,* or *In These Times.* For a more conservative perspective, you might suggest they read *The National Review* or *American Spectator.* Then have them meet with you as they prepare their speeches to discuss the following questions:

1. What is the central argument in each article?

2. What are the assumptions and biases of each article?

3. What is your reaction to these assumptions and biases?

4. How can you adapt these assumptions and biases to your own perspective and to that of your audience?

If time permits, this is also an excellent activity to conduct with the entire class.

Activity 14:

Using Television to Illustrate Viewpoints

To help ESL students gain an understanding of some assumptions that "typical" American students might have concerning controversial issues, have your ESL students watch a news broadcast such as *MacNeil/Lehrer Newshour, Firing Line,* or *Face the Nation.* As they watch these broadcasts, they should consider the following questions:

1. What are the issues being discussed?

2. What are the different perspectives on these issues?

3. Are these issues relevant in your native country? Why or why not?

Activity 15:

Advertisements and Cultural Assumptions

As with native speakers of English, ESL students can benefit from considering how advertisers adapt to their audiences. If you choose to do Application Exercise 1 from Chapter 5 of *The Art of Public Speaking,* have your ESL students consider if the five advertisements would be typical or appropriate in their native countries. Ask them to explain why they would or would not be typical or appropriate. If the advertisements would be atypical or inappropriate, ask your ESL students to explain how similar products might be advertised in their native countries.

Activity 16:

Exploring Cultural Assumptions

This activity encourages ESL students to compare the conventional assumptions regarding age, gender, religion, and the like in their native cultures with those of a "typical" U.S. audience. If you choose to do Application Exercise 2 from Chapter 5 of *The Art of Public Speaking,* ask your ESL students to write a brief paragraph explaining how they might adjust their specific purpose and message according to the demographic characteristics of a similar audience in their native countries. If the topic would not be considered appropriate, ask students to develop a topic that would be appropriate for that audience.

Activity 17:

Audience Analysis and Adaptation Worksheet

Have your ESL students fill in the Audience Analysis and Adaptation Worksheet from the Additional Exercises and Activities section of Chapter 5 in the *Instructor's Manual*. First, ask them to fill out one sheet for your public speaking class. Second, ask them to fill out a second worksheet for a hypothetical group of college students in their native countries. Ask them to reflect on the following questions:

1. Would you adapt differently to students in the U.S. than to students in your native country? Explain.

2. How can you adapt to the U.S. audience in a way in which you are comfortable?

   This activity encourages ESL students to reflect upon the values and attitudes of students in their class and in their native countries. In doing so, ESL students may become aware of their own cultural attitudes and ways to adapt to their audience.

Activity 18:

Adapting Delivery to the Classroom Audience

Effective delivery can help ESL students compensate for language differences between them and their audience. ESL students who are anxious about speaking in public need to reflect on how their delivery might affect the audience. In addition, ESL students also need to realize that their delivery is something they can learn to control and improve.

Have your ESL students reflect on how they can make their delivery more audience centered. They should consider the following questions:

1. How loud should I speak for this audience in this setting?

2. How fast should I speak for this audience in this setting on this topic?

3. What sorts of gestures will help me convey my ideas?

4. Would pauses in any places create a desirable effect on my audience?

5. How can I add vocal variety to make my speech more interesting?

Activity 19:

Assessing Main Points

As mentioned in Part One, some ESL students may be comfortable with different rhetorical patterns from those common in the U.S. As a result, it may be useful for ESL students in a public speaking class to identify their purpose, main points, and supporting materials as a way to practice stating them explicitly.

Have your ESL students evaluate the specific purpose and main points of their speeches. Have them write out the specific purpose and an outline of their main points and subpoints. They should also include any supporting materials they plan to present in the speech, and they should identify all sources of their supporting materials.

As an optional assignment, you might ask your ESL students to prepare a written self-evaluation to be handed in to you. Provide them with the following questions to use as a guide as they write their self-evaluations:

1. Is the specific purpose of the speech clear?

2. Is the specific purpose appropriate for this assignment and the time limitations?

3. Does the speech develop each of the main points sufficiently?

4. Does the order of the main points make sense?

5. Does the speech support the main points with credible supporting materials?

Activity 20:

Assessing Supporting Materials

Because the methods of supporting ideas can vary from culture to culture, it can be helpful to have your ESL students evaluate the supporting materials in their speeches to make sure they are adequate for the topic and audience they are addressing. For homework, have your ESL students outline the body of their speeches, complete with supporting materials. You can then provide each student individual guidance by responding to his or her outline.

Another approach is to have all students, ESL and non-ESL alike, prepare outlines as a homework assignment. In class, set aside time in which students, working in small groups, can evaluate one another's outlines and supporting materials. Each group should respond to the following questions:

1. For each main point, are the speaker's supporting materials sufficient?

2. Are the supporting materials taken from credible sources?

3. What additional supporting materials could the speaker include to build his or her credibility?

4. What additional supporting materials could the speaker include to answer possible objections to his or her position?

Activity 21:

Assessing Persuasive Arguments

Because different cultures have different conceptions of effective persuasion, this activity gives instructors insight into their ESL students' conceptions of persuasion and creates an opportunity for them to provide feedback on effective argumentation.

Have your ESL students evaluate the purpose of their persuasive speech and identify their arguments. For homework, have them write out the purpose of their speech and an outline of the arguments. Next, have them prepare a written self-evaluation to be handed in to you. Have the students provide detailed answers to the following questions as they complete their self-evaluations.

1. Is the purpose of the speech clear? Explain.

2. Is the topic of the speech appropriate for the assignment and the time limits? Explain.

3. Do you have enough arguments for the time limit? Explain.

4. Do the arguments seem appropriate for this audience? Explain.

5. Does the order of arguments seem appropriate? Explain.

6. Do you address any counterarguments? Explain.

7. How do you support your arguments? Explain.

8. Is the support appropriate and effective for each argument? Explain.

Activity 22:

Analyzing Counterarguments

Because different cultures have different conceptions of effective persuasion, it can be helpful to acquaint ESL students with the kind of argumentation style used in the U. S. This activity is designed to help ESL students reflect on counterarguments and supporting evidence and to look beyond their own cultural perspectives. It also gives instructors insight into their ESL students' cultural perspectives and an opportunity to provide feedback on effective argumentation.

Have your ESL students create a list of objections to their positions and then follow this with a list of counterarguments that could be used in their speeches. Have them outline the kinds of evidence that would make each argument and counterargument effective. Advise them to consider the arguments and counterarguments in terms of the audience adaptation they are doing for their speeches.

Activity 23:

Phrases and Expressions Used When Supporting Ideas

Below are some useful phrases and expressions that can help your ESL students support their ideas. List them on a handout and then meet with your ESL students as a group to discuss appropriate usage. During the discussion, encourage your ESL students to ask about and/or to describe other expressions they may have heard U.S. students use. In addition, encourage your ESL students to describe differences they may have noticed between these types of expressions and those which are commonly used in their own cultures.

Giving an Explanation

"Let me explain what I mean by . . ."

"This means that . . ."

"That is, . . ."

"In other words, . . ."

Using a Scenario

"Imagine that . . ."

"Suppose that . . ."

"What if . . .?"

"Think of it as . . ."

Using an Example	*Considering Consequences*
"Let me give you an example."	"If _____, then _____ ..."
"For example, . . ."	"As a result, . . ."
"For instance, . . ."	"Therefore, . . ."

As an optional assignment, ask your ESL students to observe a class (either your public speaking course or another class) and take note of the expressions that help support the speaker's ideas. Then hold a follow-up meeting with your ESL students in which you discuss their observations.

You might also ask your ESL students to participate in a class discussion (in either your public speaking course or another class) and then write a one-page paper in which they evaluate the extent to which they were able to use these expressions and phrases listed above to support their ideas. Ask them to respond to the following questions in their papers:

1. Describe the ways in which you supported your ideas.

2. Describe how you felt about your ability to support your ideas.

3. Describe how you might have supported your ideas more effectively.

Activity 24:

Using Connectives

Because many ESL students are socialized into different public speaking patterns, they may have different perceptions about how to organize the body of a speech. Instructors need to recognize that how the body of a speech is organized in the U.S. may differ from how it is organized in the native cultures of their ESL students. In addition, since a well organized speech can compensate for less than native-like pronunciation, ESL students should learn that carefully organizing the body of a speech is an important compensation strategy.

Have your ESL students prepare transitions, internal previews, and internal summaries for each of the main points and subpoints in their first speech. If you have time, have the students come to your office to present their speeches. As you listen, focus on the use of connectives. If you or the students are short on time, review only the connectives with them before they give the speech. If you are really pressed for time, have the students write out their connectives and hand them in for comment before they give the speech.

As an alternative, if you have several ESL students, have them give their speeches to one another. As they listen, they should focus specifically on the connectives to make sure they make sense, seem appropriate, and help the listener follow the message. Students should provide feedback to each other on the effectiveness of the connectives.

Activity 25:

Understanding Signposts

Your ESL students may or may not be familiar with signposts. It may be useful for them to have a list of frequently used signposts based on the relationships they indicate. Prepare a handout with the following list of signposts for your ESL students. You may want to meet with them to answer questions about using signposts.

To Introduce an Item in a Series

"first"
"second"
"in the first place"
"next"
"then"
"furthermore"
"moreover"
"in addition"

"also"
"similarly"
"besides"
"as well as"
"finally"
"last"

To Introduce Examples

"for example"
"for instance"
"to illustrate"
"specifically"
"for instance"
"in particular"
"that is"
"namely"

To Compare

"also"
"similarly"
"likewise"
"in the same manner"

To Contrast

"conversely"
"even though"
"on the other hand"
"in contrast"
"nevertheless"

"still"
"however"
"yet"
"although"
"but"

To Introduce a Restatement

"that is"
"in other words"
"to put it differently"

To Conclude

"in other words"
"in short"
"in summary"
"in conclusion"
"finally"
"to sum up"

To Introduce a Result or Cause

"as a result"
"hence"
"thus"
"so"
"therefore"
"consequently"

To Show Place or Direction

"close to"
"near"
"next to"
"above"
"below"
"beyond"
"in front of"

"farther on"
"nearby"
"up"
"down"
"forward"
"backward"
"behind"

Activity 26:

Assessing Introductions and Conclusions

Because ESL students may have been socialized into different public speaking patterns, they may have different perceptions about how to begin and end a speech. Instructors need to recognize that the function and features of introductions and conclusions in the U.S. may differ from those in the cultures of their ESL students. For example, the presentation and reinforcement of main points in the introduction and conclusion may be perceived as redundant or even insulting in some cultures. Although ESL students may understand the principles presented in class, it may be difficult for them to incorporate those principles into their speeches. As a result, instructors need to provide ESL students opportunities to produce introductions and conclusions before the speeches are presented in class. This and the next activity provide such opportunities.

In this activity, ask your ESL students to watch on their own the material on introductions and conclusions from *Introductions, Conclusions, and Visuals Aids: A Videotape Supplement to The Art of Public Speaking*. Have them evaluate each introduction and conclusion with an explanation of why it is or is not effective according to the criteria presented in Chapter 9 of the textbook. Ask them to write down their ideas, or ask them to see you during office hours to talk about their reactions. As an alternative, you might ask your ESL students to watch the tape together and to discuss their reactions as a group.

Activity 27:

Drafting Introductions and Conclusions

Ask your ESL students to present a working draft of their introductions and conclusions to you either in written form or orally during your office hours. Provide feedback to them either in written form or orally. Have the students evaluate their introductions and conclusions in light of the following questions:

Introductions

1. Does my introduction gain the attention of my audience? If so, how?

2. Does my introduction lead my audience to perceive me as credible? If so, how?

3. Does my introduction state the topic of my speech? If so, where?

4. Does my introduction preview the main points of my speech? If so, where?

Conclusions

1. How will the audience know I am concluding? By my voice? By a transitional word or phrase? By my delivery?

2. Have I reinforced my main idea in the conclusion so it will be clear and memorable to this audience? How?

Activity 28:

Monitoring Language Use

Using language appropriately may be one of the greatest difficulties faced by ESL students. Many ESL students do not have the same variety of registers as native speakers. For example, they may have little or no knowledge of American slang and may thus find their classmates difficult to understand. They might also be unfamiliar with the many idioms that are used in English, and thus may even have problems understanding you. In addition, they may have difficulty with English grammar and pronunciation.

ESL students may also have problems deciding on appropriate word choice. If they misuse a word, you should not think of them as stupid or difficult. If you laugh at students who misuse language, it may inhibit their participation in class. It is important to be as encouraging and helpful as possible. Try to provide appropriate words or models of grammar when possible. There are several ways you might do this depending on the needs of your ESL students and the nature of the assignment.

One approach is to have your ESL students present their speeches to you during office hours before presenting them in class. You may want to decide beforehand what kinds of language difficulties you will listen for, or you may choose to pick those items that most interfere with comprehensibility. It is not a good idea to stop an ESL student every time he or she makes a grammar error or mispronounces a word. It is usually better to discuss the errors after the speech is delivered.

Rather than having your ESL students deliver their speeches to you, you can have them deliver them to a native English-speaking classmate or to an English-speaking friend. As this person listens, he or she should write down words that the speaker has difficulty pronouncing. The ESL student should note the correct pronunciation and then practice the words he or she has mispronounced. The student should be encouraged to tape record herself or himself and then listen to the tape for pronunciation problems and overall comprehensibility.

Activity 29:

Self-assessment of Pronunciation and Grammatical Problems

Find out if your ESL students can identify their problems of pronunciation and grammar usage. For example, Japanese students often know that they have difficulty pronouncing the / r / and / l / sounds and thus, may say "led" when they mean "red." In addition, since there are no articles ("a," "an," or "the") in the Japanese language, students from Japan may mix up the definite and indefinite articles in English, or omit them altogether.

Ask your ESL students to attend to their pronunciation and grammar problems as they practice their speeches alone or with you. Decide beforehand what problems students will focus on. If students have to solve too many problems at once, they will be unable to monitor themselves effectively. However, if they focus on one or two problems, they may be more successful.

Activity 30:

Speaking Spontaneously and Maintaining Eye Contact

This activity is designed to help ESL students get used to talking while maintaining eye contact. It also gives them an opportunity to feel more comfortable speaking to a single person before they are expected to speak in front of a larger audience.

1. Ask your students to arrange their chairs in two lines facing each other.

2. Instruct those seated in one line to talk about a topic they are interested in for two minutes, speaking directly to the listener sitting opposite. The speaker should look at the listener from time to time. The listener should nod, look at the speaker, and show interest, but should not talk.

3. At the end of two minutes, all the speakers should move to the next seat so they will have new listeners. This time they should talk on the same topic for a minute and a half.

4. Then have the two lines reverse roles. Provide a new topic. Tell the former listeners to act as speakers with two different listeners.

Activity 31:

Facial Expressions and Gestures

Discuss the following question: How do facial expressions and gestures reflecting emotions vary from culture to culture?

Place your students in groups of three or four. Pass out slips of paper with the following emotions listed on each slip. Instruct the students to act out the emotion using appropriate gestures.

anger	excitement
frustration	concern
anxiety	enjoyment

Activity 32:

Nonverbal Gestures

Divide the class into groups of four to five students each. Ask students to generate as many ways as they can to express the following messages nonverbally. ESL students should be encouraged to demonstrate the common nonverbal gestures that would be appropriate in their cultures.

I'm hungry.	Good luck.
I'm not feeling well.	It's okay.
Come here.	That's very expensive.
Yes, I agree.	I can't hear you.
No, I disagree.	Be quiet.
I don't know.	It's time to leave.
Wait a second.	Stop!
You did a great job.	Calm down.

Activity 33:

Individual Delivery Practice Techniques

Having ESL students practice their speeches is critical not only to improving their delivery, but also to helping them feel confident about their use of spoken English. This activity presents three proven approaches to assisting ESL students with rehearsing their speeches.

First, strongly encourage your ESL students to tape record their speeches as they practice. As they listen to their tapes, they should focus on vocal aspects of delivery such as rate, volume, vocal variety, and pronunciation. If they know they have problems with particular words, they should listen for those words and try to concentrate on the correct pronunciation. ESL students should also practice in front of a mirror or in front of native-speaking friends. This is useful for students to get feedback on verbal and nonverbal aspects of their speeches.

Second, ESL students should set up a time with you during your office hours to present their speeches. Before they begin, ask them what they are most concerned about in terms of their delivery. If they do not know, tell them that you will respond to their delivery according to what you see fit. If students have multiple problems, let them know they have a lot to work on and should focus on one or two aspects of delivery at a time.

Third, explain the following delivery practice techniques for your ESL students:

After you have prepared your speech, select one section of the speech, such as the introduction or a main point. Practice delivering that part of your speech in front of a mirror several times. The first time, focus on the nonverbal elements discussed in class, such as eye contact and posture. The second time, focus on your rate of speech and volume. The third time, focus on vocal variety. The fourth time, pay attention to sounds or words that are problematic. The fifth time, deliver that section of the speech and combine as many elements as possible. Repeat this with other parts of the speech. Gradually deliver the whole speech.

Activity 34:

Group Delivery Practice

Because ESL students may feel anxious about speaking in public, especially in front of native speakers of English, this activity gives them an opportunity to present a short speech in a safe and more controlled environment.

Divide the class into groups of four or five students each. Have students present a three-to-four-minute speech on a topic of their choice to the other members of their group. These speeches can be impromptu or planned ahead of time. If the class is large enough so that students will not disturb each other, have the presenter stand in front of the group. If not, the presenter can sit and deliver the speech.

Activity 35:

Videotaped Delivery Practice

ESL students can learn a great deal about themselves as public speakers by watching themselves on videotape. If possible, videotape their speeches during the first round of presentations. If students want to watch their tapes at home, have them bring in their own videotape. Otherwise, make the videotape available in the audiovisual services center on campus. Give students the following list of questions to focus on as they watch themselves on videotape.

1. Evaluate your introduction based on the four objectives discussed in the textbook.

2. Evaluate your conclusion based on the two objectives discussed in the textbook.

3. Evaluate the organization of your speech. What pattern of organization did you use and why?

4. Evaluate your use of connectives. Identify each connective and its purpose in your speech.

5. Evaluate your use of supporting materials. Identify the types of supporting materials you used and explain why each was or was not appropriate for your audience. What could you have done better?

6. Evaluate your use of visual aids. How could your aids have been more effective? How effective were you in using the aids? What could you have done better?

7. Evaluate your delivery. How effective was your volume? Rate? Vocal variety? Use of gestures? Did you use any behaviors that were distracting? How could you improve your delivery for this speech if you were to present it again?

8. Based on your evaluation of your delivery, what do you think you most need to work on for your next speech?

9. In what ways did watching yourself help you become a more effective speaker?

Activity 36:

Delivery Practice with Visual Aids

ESL students may not only be anxious about presenting a speech in public, but may also be unsure of how to create a visual aid for a speech. This activity is meant to give your ESL students an opportunity to speak with a visual aid in a safe environment in which they can receive feedback about the effectiveness of their visual aid. This may help build their confidence for speaking in public, as well as for developing effective visual aids.

Have your ESL students prepare visual aids for one of their speeches. Divide the class into groups of four to five students. Have each student explain his or her visual aids. Ask the group to provide feedback on what is effective about the visual aids and about how they might be improved. Each student should have a turn to present his or her aids and to receive feedback about them.

Activity 37:

Phrases and Expressions Used When Taking Turns

Some ESL students may be unaware of phrases and expressions that U.S. students use when turn-taking, exchanging opinions, and leading a group discussion. This activity will deal with turn-taking during small-group discussions, while the next two activities will deal with exchanging opinions and leading a discussion.

Below are some useful phrases and expressions that may help your ESL students become better at taking turns when speaking in a small group. List them on a handout and then meet with your ESL students as a group to discuss appropriate usage. During the discussion, encourage your ESL students to ask about and/or to describe other expressions they may have heard U.S. students use. Also encourage them to describe differences they may notice between these expressions and those commonly used in classrooms in their own cultures.

Getting Attention

"Can I make a suggestion?"

"May I ask a question?"

"Have you considered . . . ?"

"I have a question . . ."

Interrupting

"Excuse me, but . . ."

"Pardon me, but . . ."

"Sorry to interrupt, but . . ."

"Excuse me for interrupting, but . . ."

Keeping Your Turn

"Excuse me, I'd just like to finish my point."

"Just a second, I'm almost finished."

"Please wait a second."

"Just let me finish this thought."

Continuing After an Interruption

"Anyway, . . ."

"As I was saying, . . ."

"In any case, . . ."

"Back to what you were saying . . ."

To reinforce these phrases and expressions, give your ESL students an optional assignment in which they observe a small-group discussion (in your public speaking class or in another class) and take note of the expressions that U.S. students use to take turns during the discussion. You may want to hold a follow-up meeting with your ESL students in which you discuss their observations.

Another option might be to ask your ESL students to participate in a class discussion and then write a one-page paper in which they evaluate the extent to which they were able to use the expressions listed above to take turns during the discussion. In their papers they should:

1. Describe the ways in which they took turns during the discussion.

2. Describe how they feel about their ability to take turns during the discussion.

3. Describe how they might have been more successful at taking turns during the discussion.

Activity 38:

Phrases and Expressions Used When Exchanging Opinions

Below are some useful phrases and expressions that may help your ESL students become better at exchanging their opinions when speaking in a small group. List these expressions on a handout and then meet with your ESL students as a group to discuss appropriate usage. During the discussion, encourage your ESL students to ask about and/or to describe other expressions they may have heard U.S. students use. In addition, encourage them to describe differences they may notice between these expressions and those commonly used in classrooms in their own cultures.

Asking for an Opinion

"What do you think of . . . ?"

"How do you feel about . . . ?"

"What's your opinion of . . . ?"

Disagreeing

"I don't really agree with you."

"I'm not sure I agree with you."

"I'm afraid I disagree because . . ."

"Yes, that may be true, but . . ."

Giving an Opinion

"In my opinion . . ."

"Personally, I think that . . ."

"It seems to me that . . ."

Expressing Reservation

"Yes, but . . ."

"Possibly, but . . ."

"Yes, but the problem is . . ."

Agreeing

"That's right."

"You're right."

"I think so, too."

"I definitely agree."

Emphasizing a Point

"It seems to me that the real issue is . . ."

"I think the basic cause is . . ."

"As far as I can see, the main problem is . . ."

To reinforce these phrases and expressions, give your ESL students an optional assignment in which they observe a small-group discussion (in either your public speaking class or another class) and take note of the expressions that U.S. students use when exchanging opinions during the discussion. You may want to hold a follow-up meeting with your ESL students in which you discuss their observations.

Another option might be to ask your ESL students to participate in a small-group discussion and then write a one-page paper in which they evaluate the extent to which they were able to use the expressions listed above to exchange opinions during the discussion. In their papers they should:

1. Describe the ways they exchanged opinions during the discussion.

2. Describe how they felt about their ability to exchange opinions during the discussion.

3. Describe how they might have been more successful at exchanging opinions during the discussion.

Activity 39:

Phrases and Expressions Used When Leading a Discussion

Below are some useful phrases and expressions that may help your ESL students become better at leading a small-group discussion. List them on a handout and then meet with your ESL students as a group to discuss appropriate usage. During the discussion, encourage your ESL students to ask about and/or to describe other expressions they may have heard U.S. students use. Also encourage them to describe differences they may notice between these types of expressions and those commonly used in classrooms in their own cultures.

Getting Started

"Okay, are we ready to get started?"

"Is everyone ready to begin?"

Bringing People into the Discussion

"What do you think?"

"Do you have anything to add?"

"Would you like to add anything?"

Clarifying

"I'm not sure we all understand."

"I'm not following you."

"Could you explain that again?"

Keeping the Discussion Moving

"Perhaps we should go on to the next point."

"We're almost out of time; let's move on."

"Are there any more comments?"

Encouraging Everyone to Participate

"So, would you like to comment on that?"

"What do you think about that point?"

Controlling People Who Talk Too Much

"Let's hear what some other people have to say."

"Does anyone else want to comment on this?"

"What does the rest of the group think?"

Keeping the Discussion on the Subject

"That's interesting, but it raises a different point."

"Can we come back to that point later?"

"Perhaps we should finish this point first."

Reaching Agreement and Summing Up

"Do we agree that . . . ?"

"So, to sum up, we've decided . . ."

"Let's see if we all agree."

To reinforce these phrases and expressions, give your ESL students an optional assignment in which they observe a small-group discussion (in either your public speaking class or another class) and take note of the expressions that U.S. students use when leading a discussion. You may want to hold a follow-up meeting with your ESL students in which you discuss their observations.

Another option might be to ask your ESL students to lead a small group discussion and then write a one-page paper in which they evaluate the extent to which they were able to use the expressions listed above to lead a discussion. In their papers they should:

1. Describe the ways in which they led the discussion.

2. Describe how they felt about their ability to lead the discussion.

3. Describe how they might have been more successful at leading the discussion.

Part Three

SUPPLEMENTAL RESOURCES

Resources for ESL students

Matthews, Candace. *Speaking Solutions: Interaction, Presentation, Listening, and Pronunciation Skills.* Englewood Cliffs, NJ: Prentice Hall Regents. 1994.

This textbook is designed to develop the oral communication skills of intermediate through advanced ESL students in academic and professional settings. Integrating speaking, listening, and pronunciation skills, this text includes a variety of activities that encourage individual, group, and class discussions.

Tillitt, Bruce and Newton Bruder, Mary. *Speaking Naturally: Communication Skills in American English.* New York: Cambridge University Press. 1985.

This book is designed for intermediate and high intermediate ESL students who are interested in using English in social interactions with Americans.

Porter, Patricia and Grant, Margaret. *Communicating Effectively in English: Oral Communication for Non-native Speakers.* Belmont, CA: Wadsworth Publishing Company. 1992.

This book is designed to help non-native speakers become effective listeners and speakers in interpersonal, small group, and large group contexts. The activities, examples, and assignments help students sharpen their interview, discussion, and public speaking skills.

Kayfetz, Janet and Smith, Michaele. *Speaking Effectively: Strategies for Academic Interaction.* Boston, MA: Heinle & Heinle Publishers. 1992.

This book teaches strategies for speaking in academic settings so ESL students can interact appropriately. Students learn to predict scenarios based on situation and audience, to modify their speech in reaction to other speakers' responses, and to open and close conversations depending on various contexts.

Handschuh, Jeanne and Simounet de Gergel, Alma. *Improving Oral Communication: A Pronunciation Oral-Communication Manual.* Englewood Cliffs, NJ: Prentice Hall Regents. 1985.

This book concentrates on those pronunciation problems that can cause faulty communication. The exercises provide opportunities for ESL students to use English in various social situations through carefully constructed, natural-sounding dialogues, guided practice, and free conversation.

Resources for Instructors

Books about Intercultural Communication

Asante, Molefi K. and Gudykunst, William B. (eds.). *Handbook of International and Intercultural Communication.* Newbury Park, CA: Sage Publications. 1989.

This collection of essays overviews the major theoretical and applied issues in the study of international, intercultural, and development communication. Topics include language and intergroup communication, cultural dimensions of nonverbal communication, the role of interpersonal power on intercultural communication, interracial workplace encounters, and intercultural communication training.

Gudykunst, William B. and Kim, Young Yun. *Communicating with Strangers: An Approach to Intercultural Communication, 2nd ed.* New York: McGraw-Hill. 1992.

This book provides an excellent theoretically grounded introduction to major issues in the study of intercultural communication. The authors' approach to their subject as a form of communication with strangers gives this book a unique conceptual grounding.

Hall, Edward T. *Beyond Culture.* New York: Anchor Press. 1976.

This seminal book describes the role that culture plays as a selective screen between people and their worlds. Through his concepts of high- and low-context communication, Hall illustrates what people choose to attend to as well as what they ignore in their communication.

Kim, Young Yun and Gudykunst, William B. (eds.). *Theories in Intercultural Communication.* Newbury Park, CA: Sage Publications. 1988.

This collection of essays presents current approaches to the study of intercultural communication, including constructivist theory, coordinating management theory, convergence theory, adaptation in intercultural relationships, intercultural transformation, and network theory.

Lustig, Myron W. and Koester, Jolene. *Intercultural Competence: Interpersonal Communication Across Cultures*. New York: Harper Collins. 1993.

Engagingly written and illustrated with a wealth of practical examples, this book effectively introduces readers to the basic topics central to intercultural communication in the modern world.

Samovar, Larry A. and Porter, Richard E. (eds.). *Intercultural Communication: A Reader,* 3rd ed. Belmont, CA: Wadsworth Publishing Company. 1991.

This collection of essays describes sociological and psychological factors that influence communication among people of different cultures. Providing theoretical and practical information on understanding intercultural communication, these essays focus on co-cultures in the United States and globally. Topics include the role of gender on communication, nonverbal communication, and perceptions of effective persuasion.

Samovar, Larry A. and Porter, Richard E. *Communication Between Cultures.* Belmont, CA: Wadsworth Publishing Company. 1991.

A broad-based introduction to intercultural communication, this basic text is practical and highly readable. Of special note is the chapter on communication in business, education, and health care contexts.

Ting-Toomey, Stella and Korzenny, Felipe (eds.). *Language, Communication, and Culture: Current Directions.* Newbury Park, CA: Sage Publications. 1989.

This collection of essays focuses on the relationship among language, communication, and cultures through multiple conceptual and methodological orientations. The essays look at the relationship between second language acquisition and cognition, as well as the role of language in various intercultural communication settings. A topic of interest is linguistic strategies and cultural styles for persuasion.

Books about Classroom Communication

Cazden, Courtney B. *Classroom Discourse: The Language of Teaching and Learning.* Portsmouth, NH: Heinemann. 1988.

This book brings together recent research on classroom language from all the behavioral sciences. Classrooms described include those from preschool to the university level and deal with a variety of ethnic groups within the United States and from other countries in the English-speaking world. Real children and their teachers come alive in the many transcriptions of actual classroom talk and the examples from the author's own teaching experience.

Johnson, Karen E. *Understanding Communication in Second Language Classrooms.* New York: Cambridge University Press. 1995.

This book offers an integrated view of communication in second language classrooms, a view that acknowledges the importance of what teachers and students bring to the class environment, as well as what actually occurs during face-to-face communication within the classroom.

Trueba, Henry T. *Success or Failure?: Learning and the Language Minority Student*. New York: Newbury House. 1987.

This book focuses on the academic, social, and cultural factors that inhibit learning among language minority students in school and offers ways of promoting academic success for all language minority students.

Campus Resources

Most large colleges and universities have a variety of resources for ESL students. Try contacting the office of international programs or the office of international students to ask for information about services for ESL students. Some schools have tutoring services or informal conversation groups for ESL students. Yours may even have a center for English as a second language that offers ESL courses. Be an advocate for your ESL students. If you feel you are unable to help them with their specific communication difficulties, try to find other resources at your school for the assistance they need.

Endnotes

1 Concha Delgado-Gaitan, "Traditions and Transitions in the Learning Process of Mexican Children: An Ethnographic View," in George Spindler and Louise Spindler (eds.), *Interpretive Ethnography of Education: At Home and Abroad* (Hillsdale, NJ: Lawrence Erlbaum, 1987), pp. 333-359.

2 Karen E. Johnson, *Understanding Communication in Second Language Classrooms* (New York: Cambridge University Press, 1995), p. 39.

3 Robert B. Kaplan, "Cultural Thought Patterns in Intercultural Education," *Language Learning*, 16 (1966), 1-20.

4 Edward T. Hall, *Beyond Culture* (New York: Anchor Books, 1976), p. 57.

5 Peter Avery and Susan Ehrlich, *Teaching American English Pronunciation* (New York: Oxford University Press, 1992), pp. 111-157.